by Dianne Danzig, R.N.   illustrated by Debbie Tilley

BABIES
Don't Eat Pizza

A Big Kids' Book
About Baby Brothers and Baby Sisters

DUTTON CHILDREN'S BOOKS

For Dan, Christopher, and Peter—D.D.

With love to my daughter Gillian—D.T.

With special thanks to Donna Brooks, Michele Coppola, Alissa Heyman, and Maureen Sullivan for their vision and enthusiasm

Hats off and many, many thanks *to those who helped with this book:*

Nancy Bausom, librarian, bookseller, The Storyteller Children's Bookstore, Lafayette, CA; Robin Calo, RN, MS, PNP, parent and sibling educator, Alta Bates Summit Medical Center, Berkeley, CA; Stevan Cavalier, MD, FAAP, pediatrician, Kaiser Permanente Medical Center, Walnut Creek, CA; Sue Crawford, teacher, Sleepy Hollow Elementary, Orinda, CA; Mary Danzig, grandmother, Oakland, CA; Joan Davis, Coordinator of Women's Services and Education, Alta Bates Summit Medical Center, Berkeley, CA; Colleen DeLine, teacher, reading specialist, Acres Green Elementary, Littleton, CO; Chase DeLine, big brother, Littleton, CO; Patricia Francis, MD, pediatrician, Lamorinda Pediatrics, Lafayette, CA; Douglas Fredrick, MD, Assistant Professor of Opthamology, University of California at San Francisco, San Francisco, CA; Catherine Farrell, mother, Orinda, CA; Jennifer Friedman, teacher, The Orinda Preschool, Orinda, CA; Patricia Geraghty, RN, NP, MS, Nurse Practitioner, Family and Women's Health, Walnut Creek, CA; Anne Glarner, mother, Orinda, CA; Linda Glaser, children's book author and educator, Duluth, MN; Kristi Grover, ECE, teacher, The Nurtury Preschool, Moraga, CA; Marlene Gunther, teacher, Hope Christian Academy, Littleton, CO; Linda Higham, owner, The Storyteller Children's Bookstore, Lafayette, CA; Elisa Kleven, children's book author and illustrator, Albany, CA; Mia Kleven, big sister, Albany, CA; Sharyn Larsen, former co-owner, The Storyteller Children's Bookstore, Lafayette, CA; Robin Ludmer, MLS, teacher-librarian, Beach Elementary, Piedmont, CA; Abbey Massie, mother, Lafayette, CA; Mae McGregor, grandmother, Littleton, CO; Nancy Medbery, ME, Principal, Robert E. Willett Elementary, Davis, CA; Jerri Meyerpeter, aunt, San Diego, CA; Silvi Otsmaa, mother, Orinda, CA; Mikk Otsmaa, big brother, Orinda, CA; Elizabeth Partridge, children's book author, Berkeley, CA; Vicki Perna, RN, BSN, Sibling Class Nurse Educator, Los Altos, CA; Anita Scalise, teacher, Wagner Ranch Elementary, Orinda, CA; Joseph Scalise, big brother, Orinda, CA; Ryan Sullivan, younger brother, Orinda, CA; Ann Tipton, MD, pediatrician, Kaiser Permanente Medical Center, Oakland, CA; Marc Usatin, MD, pediatrician, Lafayette, CA; Peyton Ward, big sister, Laguna Beach, CA; Carol Wiele, mother, Latrobe, CA; Erik and Bryce Wiele, big brothers, Latrobe, CA; Sarah Wilson, children's book author and illustrator, Danville, CA; and the artistic, editorial, and publishing staff at Dutton Children's Books: publisher, Stephanie Lurie, and book designer, Irene Vandervoort, whose hard work made this book possible.

*Thanks, also, to the many other families and friends who offered support and shared their new baby experiences, including those in the Sibling Classes at Alta Bates Summit Medical Center, Berkeley, CA, and John Muir Medical Center, Walnut Creek, CA.

*Special baby brothers and sisters born during the production of this book: Chad DeLine, Ben Kleven, Kai Otsmaa, McKenna Scalise, and Erin Grace Wiele.

DUTTON CHILDREN'S BOOKS
A division of Penguin Young Readers Group
Published by the Penguin Group • Penguin Group (USA) Inc., 375 Hudson Street, New York, New York 10014, U.S.A. • Penguin Group (Canada), 90 Eglinton Avenue East, Suite 700, Toronto, Ontario M4P 2Y3, Canada (a division of Pearson Penguin Canada Inc.) • Penguin Books Ltd, 80 Strand, London WC2R 0RL, England • Penguin Ireland, 25 St Stephen's Green, Dublin 2, Ireland (a division of Penguin Books Ltd) • Penguin Group (Australia), 250 Camberwell Road, Camberwell, Victoria 3124, Australia (a division of Pearson Australia Group Pty Ltd) • Penguin Books India Pvt Ltd, 11 Community Centre, Panchsheel Park, New Delhi - 110 017, India • Penguin Group (NZ), 67 Apollo Drive, Rosedale, North Shore 0632, New Zealand (a division of Pearson New Zealand Ltd) • Penguin Books (South Africa) (Pty) Ltd, 24 Sturdee Avenue, Rosebank, Johannesburg 2196, South Africa • Penguin Books Ltd, Registered Offices: 80 Strand, London WC2R 0RL, England

Library of Congress Cataloging-in-Publication Data
Danzig, Dianne.
Babies don't eat pizza : the big kids' book about baby brothers and baby sisters / by Dianne Danzig ; illustrated by Debbie Tilley.—1st ed.
p. cm.
ISBN 978-0-525-47441-8
1. Infants—Juvenile literature. 2. Brothers and sisters—Juvenile literature. I. Tilley, Debbie. II. Title.
HQ774.D27 2009
649'.10245—dc22   2008013882

Published in the United States by Dutton Children's Books, a division of Penguin Young Readers Group
345 Hudson Street, New York, New York 10014
www.penguin.com/youngreaders

Designed by Irene Vandervoort

Manufactured in China   First Edition
20 19 18 17 16 15 14 13 12 11

Not so long ago, you were a tiny baby . . .

. . . And when you were born, you stretched your arms and legs, and you gave a little cry with your very first breath. Then your parents hugged you close, and smiled their biggest smiles. How soft and cuddly you were. At last, after waiting for so long, your parents had YOU—their precious baby.

Now another baby is joining your family, and soon you'll be a big brother or big sister. Congratulations! Get ready—new babies bring lots of changes and surprises. What changes? What surprises? Let's find out.

IN THE BEGINNING

A Womb to Grow in...

Babies start out smaller than an ant. Curled up inside their moms, they grow in the uterus, or womb, a special place for babies *below* moms' stomachs. (It's not where moms' food goes.) Your baby sister or brother is growing in there. You lived there once, too.

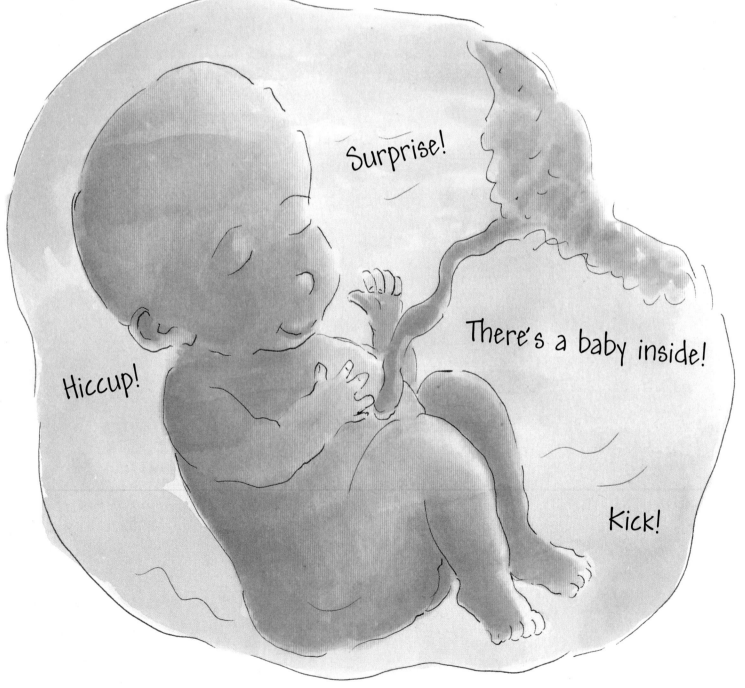

And Do Somersaults

Babies do gymnastics. One, two, or even up to seven busy babies can stretch, twist, and kick while they're inside.

And how do they eat and breathe? Air and tiny specks of food travel through the umbilical cord—a soft, twisty tube that connects babies to their moms.

Here at Last

No one knows exactly when babies will be born, but moms can make a good guess.
When it's time, someone special will take care of you. Your parents may leave
for the hospital to give birth, or go to pick your baby up, if your family's adopting.
When they come back, you'll be together again—with your new baby.

What will your baby look like? Tiny! Like when you were first born. Peek at pictures
of when you were little. How did you look? How have you changed?

Special Delivery

So how are babies born?

They're pushed out—through an opening between moms' legs, or lifted out—through a cut made in moms' tummies by their doctors. (Those moms have surgery and get a special medicine so it won't hurt.)

You were born one of those ways, and so will your baby.

And what do new babies look like?

Your Basic Baby

What color are your baby's eyes?
Even that can change. You'll know
by your baby's first birthday.

No tears yet, but babies do cry.
No teeth either.

Big head with small body.

Wacky hair.
It can fall out and
grow back in a different color.

Where's the belly button? It's hiding under the umbilical cord. That last little piece of the cord will fall off soon, then your baby's belly button will peek out. Some belly buttons turn in and some stay out.

Some babies look furry. That fine, silky hair falls off after a while.

Fingernails and toenails are short, long, or in-between. How about a manicure?

Newborns wear jewelry.

WHAT NEW BABIES LOOK LIKE

Funny Faces and Wacky Hair

Babies can look different than baby dolls. Their heads may be shaped like upside-down ice-cream cones, with splotchy or puffy faces. But soon, their heads are rounder and look better. By the way, it's fine if you touch your baby's head. Just be gentle.

And some babies look like rock stars! Fuzzy or curly, straight or swirly; a lot, a little, or none at all. Babies' hair grows every which way.

Just Peachy

Newborns change color. Their skin can grow darker, or turn golden yellow for a time. They can have spots, marks, and dots, in white, yellow, blue, or pink. Some stay, others disappear.

Their skin can be peely—like an onion, or wrinkly—like a raisin, or fuzzy—like a peach. Before long, though, their skin becomes soft and smooth.

Your dolls and stuffed animals stay the same, but your baby will grow and change, just like you.

Now, what do babies do?

WHAT BABIES DO

sleepyheads

Early on, babies mostly eat, sleep, cry, and have their diapers changed. Babies are the best sleepers in the world—most of the time. Growing and learning makes them tired and hungry.

Newborns often sleep in bassinets—beds like miniature shopping carts. In the hospital, sick or extra-small babies sleep in cozy, warm incubators (special beds that help them feel better). Incubators look like fish tanks on wheels—without the water and fish, of course.

Snack Time

New babies don't eat pizza—or ice cream—or even baby food. They don't have teeth, and their stomachs aren't grown up enough for big-kids' food.

So what do you feed a hungry newborn? Milk from moms' breasts (that's called nursing), or breast milk or formula from a bottle.

You can help feed your baby, or snuggle in while your baby nurses.

Baby Burritos

Babies can't do as much as you. And although they're little, they're a lot of work. You can help your parents, if you like. Get a diaper, help wrap your baby up like a burrito, turn on a music box, or play with your baby.

Playtime

Sleepy newborns play by watching and listening. Give a rattle or your finger to hold, play pat-a-cake, show a toy, or read a story. Babies like when you sing softly and speak quietly to them. As your baby gets older, you'll play in even more fun ways.

Baby Talk

How can someone so tiny and so helpless be so loud? Newborns are noisy. They grunt, squeak, burp, cough, sneeze, and cry. It can be annoying, but babies need to cry to get attention. Crying is babies' way of talking. What are they saying?

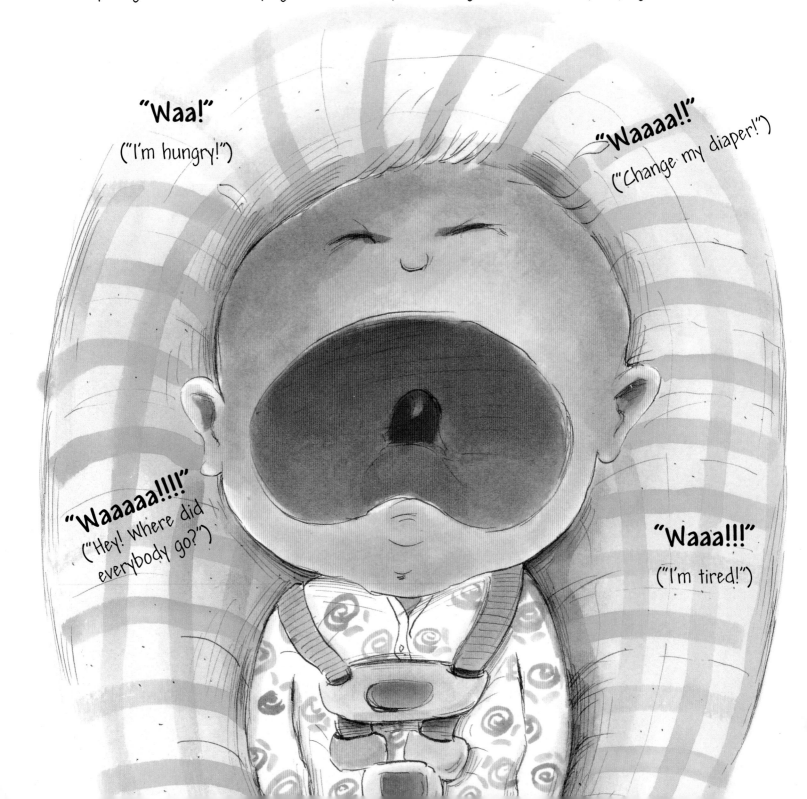

Wiggle and Squiggle

Younger babies turn and squirm, while older babies are wiggle worms. Babies like to be gently cuddled.

You can carefully hold your baby with a grown-up's help. Always sit down, rest your baby on your lap, with one hand on your baby's head and the other around your baby's back. Hold on tight—and don't be surprised if someone takes your picture. Smile!

Super Baby

Babies are small and fragile and strong. Their hands close tight around whatever they reach. Watch out for your ears and nose, and don't let your hair get too close. And if your baby grabs your hair, expect that even if you say "Stop!"—your baby won't let go. Babies don't understand your words yet and don't mean to hurt you.

Time for a Change

Babies don't mind their manners. They don't say "Please" or "Thank you," and they don't say "How do you do?" They suck on their toes, and don't blow their nose. They drool, dribble, and burp; spit up, smack, and slurp; and they dirty their diapers! Hold your nose—something's stinky!

Babies suck on anything near. Sucking makes them happy and helps them learn. Remember, though, babies choke easily, so tell a grown-up if something's in your baby's mouth.

Babies on the Go

Babies are explorers. The older they are, the more they move and the more they do. Babies are wobbly! You can help your baby, if you want. Can you believe you had to learn to roll over, sit up, and walk?

Babies are curious, too. They discover things—like buttons, beads, and bugs; taste things—like your dog's water—yuck! touch things—like Mom's lipstick and Dad's glasses; and topple everything.

So what do babies like?

WHAT BABIES LIKE

"Dada, dada, dada, dada, dada…"

Sticky, Gooey, Messy, Mushy

Babies like to learn. They try new noises, and squeal, coo, and babble. Then they say made-up words. Later, they say words you understand, like "dada," or a *special name for you.*

They learn to drink from a cup, and eat tiny bites of soft foods, like mashed bananas. After that, they try baby crackers or circle cereal. They smear their food everywhere—hands, face, hair—and, maybe, on you!

Splish, Splash, Take a Bath

It's bath time! Newborns have sponge baths (baths without a bathtub). They're sponged off to get clean.

Then—water, water, everywhere! Older, slippery, squirmy babies take their baths while sitting on towels or big sponges, in tiny tubs, or in the sink. You can help. Babies like to play while they bathe, so bring along your rubber ducky.

Babies Like to Boogie

Babies are copycats. They like to do what you do, and they like music and dancing. Bouncing is one way babies dance. Show your baby how to clap, shake a rattle, or beat a drum, and your baby will copy you. You can be in a band together! Turn on some music, bang on some pots, and boogie!

Wink, Wave, Smile, Clap

Make a silly face, say silly sounds, and hear your baby laugh. Babies like to play and be silly, especially with you. Play peekaboo, read a story, or build castles in the sand. In time, you'll play bigger kids' games. Together, you'll have more and more fun.

"Peekaboo, I see you!"

Now, enough about babies.
Let's talk about you.

THE ONE AND ONLY YOU

All Grown Up

Look how much you've grown since you were a baby. You were little, and now you're big. You learned to walk, talk, and put on your clothes all by yourself.

And, since you're more grown up, you can be a big sister or big brother. That's important. Stand up, take a bow! Hooray for you!

Love You Forever

Everyone's busy when a new baby comes. Kids and grown-ups can feel tired or left out.
But remember, your parents love you just the way you are. They always will. There is only one you, and there will never be anyone else exactly like you. After your baby comes home, you'll still get hugs and kisses, and you'll still be as special to your parents as you are now.

Timbuktu or Kalamazoo?

Kids feel all different ways about their new baby brothers and sisters, and that's okay. Just make sure you tell your parents how you feel.

And no matter what, always be gentle with your baby.

Sometimes you might be excited to be the big sister or big brother. Sometimes you might want to act little or be a baby again. Sometimes you might want your parents to send your baby far, far away (but you know they won't).

They Grow So Fast (Parents' Tips)

Dear Parents,

Adjusting to a new baby in the family can bring you and your older children closer. These tips may help. Keep the words "simple," "flexible," and "involved" in mind. Congratulations on your growing family!

1. Before your baby is born, involve your child in baby preparations, and offer your child her own pretend baby (a doll or a stuffed animal) to care for. Consider joining a sibling class with your older children.

2. Let your child know who will care for him when it's time for your baby to be born or picked up for adoption.

3. Assure your child you will be thinking of her when you're away. Leave a card, note, or photo for her when you go. Call your child while you're gone.

4. When your child visits you for the first time after your baby is born, put the baby down, hug your older child, tell him you love him, and then show the baby.

5. When you arrive home with your new baby, put the baby down, give attention to your older child, then get settled.

6. For special days, or days when others give gifts and extra attention to your baby, have small, inexpensive gifts ready for your older child. A "surprise bag" or "grab bag" works well.

7. Include your older child in daily baby-care activities. Praise ways that he helps or is involved.

8. Tell your child how much you love her for who she is. Spend one-on-one time together (without the baby) reading a story, eating a snack, playing, or chatting. Look at pictures of her when she was a baby. Talk about when she was little and why you chose her name.

9. Expect older sibling regression and mood swings. It's normal for children to have mixed feelings about their new baby brothers and baby sisters. Over time, your child will be more secure with your changed family and may even want to be the older child again!

10. Be patient with yourselves and your children. Everyone is adjusting to the changes a new baby brings.

Having a new baby and older children is work, but it gets easier. Enjoy the little things—your baby's smile, big brother's or big sister's hug, laughing at first tries and sticky messes, rocking your baby, and new successes. Your children will grow, and those memories will be cherished.

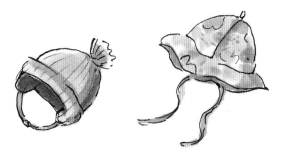

And sometimes, when your baby smiles at you—and wants to be with you and nobody else—then those times, you just might be glad that you have a baby brother or baby sister.